THE LIBRARY
ST. MARY'S COLLEGE OF MARYLAND
ST. MARY'S CITY, MARYLAND 20686

D1781468

GROCERIES

GROCERIES

HERBERT SCOTT

UNIVERSITY OF PITTSBURGH PRESS

Copyright © 1976, Herbert Scott
All rights reserved
Feffer and Simons, Inc., London
Manufactured in the United States of America

Library of Congress Cataloging in Publication Data

Scott, Herbert, birth date
  Groceries.

  (Pitt poetry series)
  I. Title.
  PS3569.C625G7   811'.5'4   76-4974
  ISBN 0-8229-3332-2 (cloth)
  ISBN 0-8229-5270-X (paper)

The author is grateful to Western Michigan University for two Faculty Research Fellowships during which many of these poems were written.

Some of the poems in this book appeared earlier in *The Back Door, The Barataria Review, Chariton Review, Poetry Northwest, Poetry Now, Skywriting,* and *The Third Coast.* They are reprinted with the permission of the editors.

"Grazing" is reprinted from *What Is That Country Standing Inside You*, published by Exploration Press, 1976. Used by permission.

*The publication of this book is supported
by a grant from the National Endowment for the Arts
in Washington, D.C., a Federal agency.*

FOR

SCOTTY · MEGAN · RANNAH · ERIN

"The Fear of Groceries" is dedicated to Stuart Dybek.

"Butcher's Dream" is dedicated to Martin Grossman.

"The Shoplifter's Handbook" is dedicated to Roger Weingarten.

CONTENTS

I   **Opening Up**
    Opening Up   3

II   **Learning the Business**
    The Childhood of a Grocer   7
    Boss   8
    Thief   9
    Butcher's Dream   10
    Boss on the Floor   11
    Boss's Dream   12
    Good Fresh Country Eggs   13
    Breakfast at Aunt Hattie's   14
    Merchandising   15
    Hamburger   16
    Red Meat   17
    Hams   18
    Six Month Review   19

III   **The Shoplifter's Handbook**
    Directions   23
    Precautions   24
    Guilt   25
    Warning   26
    Accessories   27
    Alibis   28

IV   **The Grocer's Children**
    Bag Boy   31
    Pet Foods   32
    Checker   33
    The Clerk's Dream   34
    Coffee   36
    Dairy   37
    Relief Locations Manager   38

Glassware   39
Produce's Mouse   40
Produce and Relief   41
Grazing   42
The Pig Man   44
The Waitress at Aunt Hattie's   45
Butcher's Wife   46
Boss's Father   47
Canned Goods   48
Canned Goods' Dream   49
Detail   50
The Night Crew   51
Sunday   52
The Grocer's Children   53
Boss in the Back Room   54
Closing Up   56

V **The Fear of Groceries**
The Fear of Groceries   59
Potatoes   60
Edna   61
Schooling   62
Hands   63
Pension Day   64
Widows Shopping   65
The Lost Aisles   66
Cracked Eggs   68
The Children of the Poor   69
The Homemaker   70
Home Delivery   71
Boss's Lament   72
Supper at Aunt Hattie's   73
Armed Robbery   74

OPENING UP

OPENING UP

Boss turns on one light
above the safe,
a closed fist. He kneels
to the ceremony
of money, the morning sun
edging across the street,
the first customer
knocking at the door.
Boss plants the tills,
seed money, the new crop,
clips his black bow tie
like tiny wings across
his throat, whistling
between his teeth.

Butcher slings a hindquarter
on the block,
hones his long knife.
He knows where the bones
knuckle. The red angels
on his apron turn black.
Drums of bone and fat
fill for the rendering
plant truck. Everything
reduced to profit.
The wrapper spins a new skin
around steaks and chops. Butcher
catches her up against
the meat block, pinches
her ass. A slow dance
of carcasses, lamb, beef,
hog on heavy hooks.

The checker leans
into her stall,
hands on hips,
studies a list of specials,
as the lights come on
in glassware, pet foods,
paper, household, and dairy.
Boss unlocks the automatic
door. The first customer
pulls a cart from the rack,
pushes down produce,
stands quietly for a moment,
three bright, hard lemons
in one hand.

LEARNING THE BUSINESS

THE CHILDHOOD OF A GROCER

On Saturdays my old man
give me and my brothers
each a dime
and them as wanted
hiked ten mile
to the country store
bought loaves
of fresh baked bread
quart jars of mustard
loafed the afternoon
in sycamore shade
in the haze of blue hills
rolling bread into balls
to savor the pucker
of mustard on our tongues.

BOSS

I am one of the old line.
No one give me nothing.
I earned what I earned
and stole what I stole.
I know this business

like a beetle knows shit.
You got to live in it.
You got to smell it
like the sweat under your arms.
I smell groceries everywhere I go.

I love groceries,
the women coming in
lonely as hell.
The rich, the ugly,
the beautiful, the sweet,

they all walk through
them doors.
You want a education
you come to the right place.
We all got to eat.

THIEF

A big-boned woman
heavy breasted
slips a boneless steak
in each bra cup.
Butcher grabs her
drags her back
behind the cooler.
She goes nuts,
makes him
go in, screams
bloody murder
as he pulls her breasts
out too. He slaps her
on the face
to shut her up.
"You got to get tough,
these broads,
they'll steal the pants
right off your ass."
Boss feels up the steaks,
warm as toast.
"Medium rare," he says.

BUTCHER'S DREAM

I seen a cat once,
its head pasted
to the pavement
by the wheel of a car,
but its legs don't know it,
the whole body scrambling
to get up, to get loose.
I always wished I could work
with live meat, the red salt
crusting on my wrist.
I should of been a doctor.
I used to worry
what is the tenderest part
of the human carcass.
Then I seen some cannibal said,
the palm of the hand.
A delicacy you can't find
in other game. He'd kill
for the human hand.
How do you figure?
Not even a meal.
But it makes you wonder.
It makes you look
at your own hand
like a strange animal.

BOSS ON THE FLOOR

No one knows how Boss
keeps out of jail.
Boss, cupping a buttock

as he explains the merits
of Maxwell House coffee.
Boss, brushing a nipple

reaching for Van Camps
pork and beans. Boss, excusing
himself down the narrow aisles.

Boss on his knees
stocking his hand up a leg
as he comments on the sunny weather.

BOSS'S DREAM

She come in one morning,
sassy as spring. I said,
Mam, you sure got long legs.
She smiled. I said, I bet
they come together
like the intersection
of Cedar and Vine. She said,
I bet you know the way
to get there from here.
We drove west of town,
back into Beecher's woods,
walked a quarter mile
through brush, wild grape
and onions, piled leaves under
a cottonwood shedding fur,
her legs branched out.
It was good in there.
Later, she had to take
a leak, squatted down
in the leaves and pissed
in her shoes. All the way
back to the car, her shoes
squishing, laughing to beat hell.
The best it ever was.
I'd of give her the keys to the store,
but she never come back.

GOOD FRESH COUNTRY EGGS

Forty-acre farmers bring eggs to market
in milk pail, basket, cases
layered like cakes, gathered from nests
perched high above king snakes,
skunks, egg-sucking dogs and cats;
or stolen from weeds where would-be mother hens
stash them away to hatch a family.
"Laid this morning," the farmer says.

We read the eggs by candle light,
four moons in each hand shine
translucent, clear and fresh,
someone's breakfast. "Yolks that
stand up and holler *good morning*,"
the farmer says. In others

the foetus curls, an old drunk,
suspended in liquid, does a dead man's
float. We crack them, skulls in a bucket,
stillborn children. The news travels
through your nose. "Good fresh country
eggs," the farmer says. "None of your
city eggs with crap all over.
Country chickens know how to wipe their asses."

BREAKFAST AT AUNT HATTIE'S
"We eat across the street."

The cook goes crazy once a month
every order comes up *cheeseburger*
no matter what you send in,
eggs over easy, sunny side up,
cheeseburger, short stack and sausage,
grapefruit and toast, *cheeseburger*.
The waitresses go wild
no-tip customers slamming out
like empty cash drawers.
Cook sings to herself, burners wide open,
basting in sweat, the griddle sizzling
with cheeseburgers. She runs them
through the garden, lettuce, tomato,
pickle, sweet bermuda onion, mayonnaise
and ketchup, lines them up
on the counter like hats.
Aunt Hattie shakes her head, sorrowfully,
"Good cooks is hard to find,"
praying for fifty orders
for cheeseburgers with everything.

MERCHANDISING

Butcher's knife
skins the bone
white as neon.

He doesn't throw
anything away.
No one knows

what goes in
hamburger.
Something old

he bleeds it in,
educates his customers
to use it up

before the gas
blows it up.
Butcher cuts

his chickens
on the saw.
Breasts grow attached

to the ribs,
the thigh to the back.
If he could stick

a piece of tail
to the leg
he would.

HAMBURGER

Butcher plugs
a red light
above the hamburger.
GUARANTEED GROUND
FRESH EVERY HOUR
the sign reads.

From this fountain
of light the meat drinks.
Even the fat
turns pink, now,
born again
in this world.

RED MEAT

"The counter life of fresh meat is three days."

Two days under
fluorescent lights
meat turns gray
as the skin of rats

slate-colored steaks
laid out for viewing
like dead fathers

mourners passing
shaking heads, lamenting
the high cost of survival.

The third day
we turn the other cheek,
expose a new side

you only imagined
existed. "They look
so natural," you say.

We are artists.
The flesh glows
health for another day

haloed
by a wreath
of fresh greens.

HAMS

A woman brings a ham back.
She found maggots
eating Easter dinner.

A display of twenty hams
against the wall,
fat dripping down.

Each one unwrapped finds
maggots burrowed in.
We pour Clorox on the tiles,

behind the baseboard.
Armies of maggots boil out.
Butcher wipes the hams

in vinegar, wraps them up
marked down by ten percent.
We sell them all.

SIX MONTH REVIEW

You ain't naturally gifted
in the sales and service line.
Hell, you couldn't sell
beans to a fart hound.

You got to work on your strong points.
You can spell, but too bad
you can't write worth shit,
no one can read the signs you hang.

What can you do? Work the checkstands,
stack cans, trim vegetables, sort bottles.
I suspicion you got a head
on your shoulders. Who needs it.

Don't smart ass the customers.
Sack the cans on bottom the eggs on top.
Fill the empty shelves, don't stand
around your thumbs in your belt.

Keep your apron clean and your pockets honest.
You'll make it all right, you'll live to be forty.

THE SHOPLIFTER'S HANDBOOK

DIRECTIONS

Keep your head on straight, let your eyes
be rovers. Indecision breeds suspicion.
If you know where you are going get there.

Meat puts muscle on your frame.
Endow yourself if God didn't.
A cod piece for your crotch,
a brace of filets for your chest.

Slip oysters in your pockets but not sardines.
A broken arm slings a chicken.
Fold the *News* around a steak.

Remember, good things come in small packages.
Cigarettes go up in smoke,
eye shadows disappear in purses,
pills and purges leave no trace.

PRECAUTIONS

Take only what you can conceal.
It's a free country. You may return
an empty bottle, fill up again,
become a regular customer.

Carry no identification, labels, fingerprints,
pictures of loved ones, birthmarks.
Forget your name. Remember your sex.
If you become confused,
touch yourself gently between the legs.

If you get caught,
choose a new name to plead your case:
Amanda, worthy to be loved, Manfred,
peace among men. Later you may need
Delores of sorrows, Hector holding fast.

GUILT

The time will come
you will grow a hand on your shoulder,
walk with a limp, surprise yourself
in the mirror. Disguise. Dye hair.
Fake a moth of a moustache feeding
beneath your nose. You think it's real
until it flies away.

You have a pocketful of moths, of holes,
your clothes are full of openings.
You fear that everything will show,
will come alive, chickens wing
from your arms, your body leak,
soft goods rise like kites
to string you from the ceiling.

Confession wags your tongue. Clip its tail.
You want purity and nakedness.
Give to charity what you can't use or sell.
Store up credit and good will. Begin again.

WARNING

Trust no one. You have no friends.
Your appetite empties pockets, the cost
of living balloons from your breath.
Can you walk a staight line?
No one will pass this test.

ACCESSORIES

Your children grow hands like empty plates.
Hold them upside down, they sprout
a possum pouch. Lick their snouts
until they learn to smell each other out.

Let their teachers try to pry them open.
They remain closed as apples.
Take a bite. Their eyes and mouths are white.
Chew into the seeds, you'll spit them out.

Leave them in their skins, you nurtured them.
There's nothing you can do
to change the way their fingers grow.

ALIBIS

I am your long lost son, your daughter.
Don't you remember me, Father?
My sister's sick mother's giving birth.
A catastrophe fell off the shelf into my shirt.
It's the first time I forgot to pay.
They made me do it, my starving children,
my lame dog, my drunken father
who beats me with a hose.
I want to see a priest, my dead mother,
the President. Please forgive me. Forgive me.

IV
THE GROCER'S CHILDREN

BAG BOY

Bag Boy whips
the sacks open
with one flick
of his wrist,
moving his body
like a matador,
a little dance
he does
free of charge.
He is the best
and knows it,
using both hands,
the cans leaping
into the bag
in perfect arcs,
an item for every space,
the bag packing
straight and solid,
frozen foods separate,
the bread on top.
Customers love Bag Boy.
He lets them crunch
their own potato chips.

PET FOODS

Pet Foods has a woman,
comes in every day,
wants to know the difference
between meat and meat by-products.
She leans her elbows on her cart,
one high-heeled foot hooked
on the axle. Pet Foods swears
he can hear her nylons
rubbing on her thighs
as she rocks her legs.
She wants to know
do milk bones really clean the teeth.
She's thinking about getting
another dog, she buys so much
dog food. Boss says he's going
to move Pet Foods to glassware,
pick up the sales of jellies and jam.

CHECKER

Checker is beautiful,
dark, shiny hair,
breasts gentle as mares'
noses, easy gaited.
She doesn't like it
when Pet Foods
grabs her breasts
in the back room.
She knees him in the groin.
"They think you're meat
and they're bone," she says.
But she doesn't mind Bag Boy
feeling her legs
behind the checkstand
when he reaches for the sacks.
She knows he's not serious,
just passing the time of day.

THE CLERK'S DREAM

I'm going to save
my money and someday
buy a store in the neighborhood.
Me and my wife will run it,
I'll be my own boss.
And when I take money
out of the till
it will be my money.
And I'll open when
I feel like it,
and close when I feel like it.
I'll wear a flannel shirt
and no tie, and when my kids
get home from school
they'll stock the shelves,
they'll be cute as shit
in their little aprons,
and wait on customers.
I figure I'll make
maybe twenty grand a year,
and I'll join the Junior Chamber
of Commerce, and maybe
the Lions. I'll let my wife off
one afternoon a week
to play cards with the Jaycee
Janes, and on Christmas

I'll pack a apple box
with bent cans and busted cereal,
and maybe even a turkey,
and take it to the church
to give to them less
fortunate.

COFFEE
"We grind our own."

You have to drink
coffee, or no one
survives ten o'clock.
Your shriveled eyes
are plumped up by coffee.
You do not regret
the brown stain
of moss on your teeth,
your hot tongue,
an otter swimming
the polluted river
of your throat.

Can you dream
the Amazon, the jungles
of Brazil pushed back
by coffee,
the intolerable morning sun
rising before breakfast
like a fat American,
while the hard, stained
fingers of natives
rattle you awake
to a full cup
of black coffee?

DAIRY

Dairy likes to tell
about the day
a lady found a rat
in a half gallon
of milk.
He lectures us
on the importance
of rotating
perishable merchandise,
always putting
the new product
behind existing stock,
so nothing spoils.
"Now you take
a milk rat," he says,
"let it get old
and blinky,
it can taste
purely terrible.
Wouldn't want it
on *your* table,
would you?"

RELIEF LOCATIONS MANAGER

Relief is everywhere
at once. He's on his way
up. When he works the front,
the register jumps
under his fingers,
groceries flashing past
like landscape,
his arms almost
screaming with motion.
If he comes to help you
in your section, you know
you're moving too slow.
You go home ashamed
of your thick, clumsy hands.
Relief's bucking for manager
in a new store. You hope
he'll make it.

GLASSWARE

I do the job
the best I can.
You won't find
a jar put of place.
All the labels
faced forwards,
no dust on *my* shelves,
I use the feather
twice a week.
I want to make Relief
at least before I'm thirty.
I don't know why
people don't pick up
more pickles and dressing.
We had a rainy summer,
I guess.
If you get a chance
to teach me the books,
on my own time,
I sure would appreciate
that. I had two years
at the junior college.
I'd like to learn
all I can about the business
so if something opens up
at least I can get
a handle on it.

PRODUCE'S MOUSE

One old mouse
he come every night
to climb the rack
and nibble corn.
Only the sweetest
freshest ears
would he eat. I try
to catch that mouse
seven days a week,
a year I try
but he just keep
coming up the rack
tasting the corn
like the table was set
for him. And no
poison would he touch
no trap would he spring
but like it was special
he eat the cheese
with his corn
and I never did catch
the son of a bitch.

PRODUCE AND RELIEF

Produce tends
the vegetables
like a mother

caring for
small children,
peeling the leaves

from lettuce
with the gentle touch
of comforting a hurt

and with thick fingers
caressing the veins
of a cabbage head.

Relief, like an ant,
works around Produce
as if a rock were in his way

flicking his knife
through the vegetables
with nervous intensity

never pausing
except to flip
a grape or cherry

to his mouth
his tongue curling
like a lizard's.

Yesterday, over a crate
of fresh turnips,
Produce coldcocked Relief.

GRAZING
... wearing our appetites in our eyes ...

We learn to live
off the fat of the land,
apricots pink as thumbs,
the hearts of melons
the color of tongues,
filling our mouths
with the sweet flesh
of Crenshaws, Casabas,
the delicate meat
of apples, pears, freestone
peaches. We eat our way
across America, Santa Rosa
plums, Paw Paw concords,
Indian River oranges,
the names of our ancestors
floating in the air
like pollen, Tartarian,
Coachella, D'Anjou, Thompson.
We learn the hand is a thicket
for berries, a field of peanuts,
an arbor for grapes.
Seeds litter the floor
like spent bullets.
We have survived again.

In the deserts of California
the tossing fruit is gentled
by the hands of migrants,
their transient children,

strapped into line
on the belts of conveyors,
the sun nailed shut
beneath lids of crates
shipped across America.
There is no more open range,
no wild persimmon, plum,
black raspberry. Fields
are being paid not to bear
children, crops ploughed under,
chickens and hogs bulldozed
into open pits. But here
is the hallelujah tree
dropping its fruit across
our paths. Come. Fill
your apron like a cornucopia.
Take the sun between
your teeth. Let it shout
to your tongue, a comrade in joy.

THE PIG MAN

The pig man comes
once a day to haul
the garbage. Perched high
on his throne of swill

he is the king
bringing
his heavy princesses
to roll the cans.

Oh to have girls
so thick and strong
to lift lard drums of swill
like baskets of wash!

The fat bastard
should have had sons
to be the men
his daughters are.

THE WAITRESS AT AUNT HATTIE'S

The waitress dreams
a thousand dollar tip
her own Dew Drop Inn
where the dollars
lie down in rows
like green, fertile fields.
She leans to pour
a cup of coffee,
her thoughts
and thighs tabled.
She is an oasis
in the eyes of salesmen.
Their dry mouths
water at her breasts.
They dream
the gentle sway
of boats at anchor.

BUTCHER'S WIFE

Butcher's wife
weighs 300 pounds
is crazy jealous.
Saturday nights
he gets drunk
and lays a whore.
Later, at home, his wife
pulls off his pants
and shines a flashlight
on his pecker,
sniffs it, grabs his balls
and won't let go
until he confesses,
slaps his face
to make him sober up
enough to fuck her.
Next morning
for breakfast
she fixes him
eggs and toast
and waffles
a big center slice
of fried ham.

BOSS'S FATHER

When my old man died
he fell over in the field
like a blasted stump.
They come to get him,
the sirens whining,
the high point
of his life. So dumb
he couldn't even say *ambulance*.
He told them doctors
the *avalanche* come
to carry him away.
They must of passed that story
a thousand times
around the hospital,
them nurses and them mop boys
laughing their asses off,
my old man pissing out his life
all the while. I'm telling you
there ain't no end
to the ignorance in this world.

CANNED GOODS

You get near forty
they give you cans,
the heaviest job
in the store.
They don't want you around
when you're slowing down.
They got the last one
on a heart attack.
Forty-three.
Those bastards know
what they're doing.
You either walk out
or they carry you out.
I put in for crackers and cookies.
You think I'll get it?
Not a chance.

CANNED GOODS' DREAM

When I was a kid
we bunked in one room
piled two and three a bed
the beds lined up like desks
in the country school.
I slept with my sister
closest to me. That night
I could see her eyes
move like rabbits in moonlight,
then fix on mine, knowing
I was there. I knowed
she could smell the heat climbing
from my body. Her hands
beat on my sides as I come down.
She tried to take me
without crying, her small body
tough as hickory,
but the cry come, strange
and long, as I felt her give
and fell into her
for the first time in my life.
She lay humid and warm
like a summer night,
the sky deep in stars.
Who can say we knowed any better?

DETAIL

I clean the incinerator,
ashes flying like gray birds.
"Use a paper sack
over your head
or you'll look like a ghost."
Tearing out eyes, mouth, and nose,
deliverymen laughing as they pass.

They must have burned cows in here,
the ashes of three wars,
bones from old murders, abortions,
the history of the world in strata.
I throw up in my paper sack.
"Use boxes when you can,
sacks cost money.
You sick or something?
Gray as turkey gut."

THE NIGHT CREW

We inherit
their stale morning
air, the sweat
of generation.

Bodies humped over
cases of Kotex,
Sweetheart Soap,
they feed the shelves,

those cold, thin mouths,
transient mothers,
all the long night
dreaming they are alive.

They slip out as we enter.
Later, at home, they fall
like shadows across the beds
of drawn rooms

while wide-eyed children
whisper past
the pale strangers
who sleep through their lives.

SUNDAY

Sunday morning
we go to work
before the Catholics
go to church.
We wash, we wax
the floors, trim vegetables
down, the brown leaves,
cracked stalks renewed
by water and the knife.
You could lie down
and die on the empty shelves
in the deep pit of Sunday
while somewhere women
wind their long hair,
the faces of their men
luminous in the cold
electronic light, the children
in their rooms practicing
what we already know,
all of us listening,
listening with bent heads
to the sermon of our lives.

THE GROCER'S CHILDREN

The grocer's children
eat day-old bread,
moldy cakes and cheese,
soft black bananas
on stale shredded wheat,
weeviled rice, their plates
heaped high with wilted
greens, bruised fruit,
surprise treats
from unlabeled cans,
tainted meat.
The grocer's children
never go hungry.

BOSS IN THE BACK ROOM

1.
There's too much money in groceries.
I seen it happen in my life.
The bankers in their high hats,

they own this place.
They don't care nothing about groceries.
It's paper and ink to them.

2.
I love to work the checkstands Saturdays.
The carts lined up, bulging with goods.
You weigh the produce heavy, ring the prices

high. That's where you make your wages.
Keep the customers talking. They don't know
which way their money went.

3.
I know the clerks steal.
You got to keep them happy.
Jack the prices a little,

let the customers pay.
They got their own racket,
somewheres. They take you,

you take them. Live and let live,
I always say. It ain't the worst
business in the world.

4.
Marriage, that's the travesty of your life.
You spend the rest of your days
picking the fleas out of your ears.

My wife got married so young
she don't remember her maiden name.
And the women you see come in,

day after day, they ain't stupid.
Their old man's sleeping on the couch
or out playing pig's knuckle

with the boys. I'm telling you,
this world is full of lonely women.
It's a great place to be.

CLOSING UP

The sunset like a cut throat.
The night bleeds white,

flecks of milk in its mouth,
the tongue you sing to.

Your face in the window,
looking in

a tie slung over
your shoulder like a rope.

Going home, you fall into your wife
like a torrent of stars.

THE FEAR OF GROCERIES

THE FEAR OF GROCERIES

A man goes to a grocery store to buy
a can of peaches. Returning home
and opening the can for his supper
he discovers not peaches, but a heart.
He slumps to the floor of his kitchen
holding the heart in his lap like a fish.
The label, he checks again, reads *peaches*,
he is sure, or does it say *fishes*?
He looks at the fish in his lap,
his finger hooked in its mouth.
Very much like a heart, he says.
He bends his head to cry and sees
his children's faces reflected in the red eyes
of the heart, the glossy, salmon heart.
His children are spawning,
or drowning in an ocean, their faces
very like the halves of canned peaches.

POTATOES

1.
Potatoes burn green as apples
in fluorescent light, turn
bright, shine poison.

2.
The blind baby swings low
in its mother's belly.
It does not know the damage of light,
its father holed up in a golf game,
its mother reading the refrigerator.

3.
The checker rings the dinner bell,
adding it all up.
Here is your supper, ma'am.
The girl smiles, her teeth white as semen.

EDNA

She wheels her tire
through the streets of town
in her flower-print dress
and tennis shoes.

She doesn't speak,
but smiles at everyone.
No one knows
where she lives,

who pays her wages.
At noon she stops
by the store,
parks her tire at the curb,

a B. F. Goodrich,
puts her money down
a Double Cola,
Hostess Cupcake lunch.

She lifts the bottle like a horn.
The song she plays is short.
A workman's lunch,
leaning on the plate glass

store front, driving off,
her one-wheeler
taking her down
familiar roads.

SCHOOLING

Late afternoon the children
come in from school.
All day they have eaten
the sorrow of small rooms
the tragedy of textbooks
until their stomachs spin
like the skies over battlefields.

In the sweet aisles
their empty hands
pulse like hearts
their bodies open like gates
to fill with the flood of goods.
At suppertime they founder
in the laps of their fathers.

HANDS

A man is putting on his hands.
They have grown soft as old potatoes.
He can't do a thing with them.
He found them in his neighbor's yard,
his neighbor's wife. They are old bones.
They are skin trying to make sense.
He gives them one more chance
not to make money, not to kill.
They empty his pockets. They finger him.
He is trying to remember if they are his hands.
If he puts them to his face
will they cup his eyes like pools?
Can he drink from them, will they feed him?
These hands shake in his lap,
buried in the fresh linen.
His wife took his left hand. His wife said,
I am your right hand. Which hands are his,
which body from the closet did they choose?

PENSION DAY

The tweedy faces
of old men drifting in.
Prunes and dried beans.
Old whiskered children,
their bladders bleed,
Salvation Army pants

stiffen like dogs,
the scent of treed possum.
They come from rented rooms,
eyes dark with age,
hands like moles,
to sniff for bargains.

They know they won't make it
another month, arteries hard
as nails, pockets empty,
their lives tucked away
like money in a sock,
drawing no interest.

WIDOWS SHOPPING

The widows push their carts
down worn, memorial aisles,

this house of no shadows,
lifting last year's summer

from the shelves
of glittering cans,

their own stale freshness
sealed in, like fruit picked green

for shipping, cold storage
apples out of season.

THE LOST AISLES

There are aisles
we have not discovered
where a man and woman
are making love.
We hear her calling
his name, his name
is a song falling
beneath our feet.

All who enter
the lost aisles
must walk barefoot,
must carry
what they own,
must own their voices
lifting in praise.

In the lost aisles
when the lovers
have finished
the man lies still
within the woman, waiting
for her to rouse.
She does not push
him away, but holds him

in her arms
and legs, holds him
like a tree, the fruit
still falling around them.
They may eat
without leaving
each other's bodies.

The lovers may be lost
in any aisle
we cannot discover,
they may be waiting
for us to come, gather
the fruit in our arms,
gather them in our arms.

CRACKED EGGS

"Any cracked eggs today?"
The old woman lifts her face
to me like a cratered moon.
I shake my head. Later,

in the back room,
I find her sucking
cracked eggs, a bucket
of them at her feet,

plucking the shells
from between her teeth
like the stems of strawberries,
a beard of yellow on her chin.

Surprised, she stutters an excuse,
broken speech twisting
like bones in her throat,

then hurries to the door,
old mother, wrapping
the shambles of her dignity
in the flapping wings of her coat.

THE CHILDREN OF THE POOR

The children of the poor run wild,
rape the candy counter,
pull off Baby Ruths, go down
on Butterfingers. Half-starved
they eat their way through produce,
peanut shells and grape pits
planted down the aisles,
bare knees clenched like fists,
faces ringed with sores.
The parents buy white cornmeal, beans,
sidemeat, turnip greens, lard,
cheap tokay and muscatel.

THE HOMEMAKER

She is climbing into the refrigerator,
putting her fingerprints into the butter,
tasting old onions, sleeping with the leftovers.
She is helping herself, finding the right shelf.
She is firming up like Jello, slowing
down, keeping cool, her skin thinning
into pliofilm, her flesh stiffening into steaks.
She is becoming a meal, ready to be eaten.

HOME DELIVERY

You have been here before.
She lets you in, whispers clues
in your ear, the missing
child, the dog that ate
the birthday, the bird
trapped in the refrigerator.
You reassure her, say
it doesn't matter.
But she is lonely,
and she bares her breasts,
and you take her nipples
between your teeth.
Now she remembers you,
the one who tattoos
flowers on her neck,
and she gives herself
one last time
for old times' sake.
When you leave, kicking
the mud from your boots,
you hear her calling
a name you don't remember.

BOSS'S LAMENT

This ain't no business for old men.
Look around. Show me the men
over fifty. You got to be young
and easy looking. You got to have
the glad hand and the sweet hello,
a smile as pretty as a mother's fart.

Someday I'll eat shit and not spit
it out. I'll want my job too much,
or end across the street washing dishes,
a bottle in my pants. The personality boys
will take my place. No more you don't
need to know nothing about groceries.

SUPPER AT AUNT HATTIE'S

A film of grease rises like dew,
settles an ancient dust on the faces
of regulars. Coffee thickens in their throats.
Beneath the small tables legs
shuffle together like decks of cards,
hands play out in laps like dead-end roads.

Clerks, salesmen, drifters
fold their foreign bodies
into stiff-backed chairs. No home
claims them. Their bowels empty in public,
but their nights are private.

Aunt Hattie mothers them: "You clean
your plate before you leave, you hear?"
Toothpicks dredge their teeth.
Mouths of sweat darken under arms.
Aunt Hattie smiles, the cash register sings.
"Come again when you can stay longer."

ARMED ROBBERY

1. The Stock Clerk
The last time I filled
my pants I was thirteen,
my old man booted me
through the screen door
for touching my sister
I slept with in the same
room, the same bed.
What do they expect?
I hid my trousers under
a rock next to a blackjack
oak, let them rot away.
He never got near me again,
enough to kick my ass.

But I saw his face flash
like a grease fire
in the eyes of that bandit,
and I remembered.
The gun turned in my back
like a key, everything let loose
like a gravel slide
down Black's mountain.
I only got one pair of pants
fit to work in. My wife cried
when she saw them, unlaced
my shoes to pull them down.
They'll never come clean.

2. The Checker

When he touched me
with the cold blue barrel
of that gun, I thought
my skin would part.
I never knew such heaving
since my son turning,
pushing in my womb.
It felt like birth,
the hot pulse
stroking my thighs.
I felt taken, and given.
I gave what I could,
all he asked for.
I lay down wanting
whatever death he could offer,
wanting to be pinned
like an insect, a tattoo
on his chest. I will carry
his face chiseled in me
like a stone child, a jewel.
It's something maybe
never happens to you
once in your life,
if you survive it.
I know I could
have made him happy.

3. The Manager
I didn't want to see
his face. Show me
a picture of the gun,
it weighed a thousand pounds,
had a blue complexion,
didn't have to say a word.
I knew how to feed it.
Yes, I'm glad to be alive,
say hello to my wife
and my pet rabbit,
you stupid fuckers.
You want a hero
go over to the stadium
and pay your money
like everyone else.
You can shove these keys
if you think they mean more
than a way to pay the rent.
No sir, I couldn't say
"Yessir" fast enough.
I'm in this business to stay alive.

PITT POETRY SERIES

Adonis, *The Blood of Adonis*
Jack Anderson, *The Invention of New Jersey*
Jon Anderson, *Death & Friends*
Jon Anderson, *In Sepia*
Jon Anderson, *Looking for Jonathan*
John Balaban, *After Our War*
Gerald W. Barrax, *Another Kind of Rain*
Leo Connellan, *First Selected Poems*
Michael Culross, *The Lost Heroes*
Fazıl Hüsnü Dağlarca, *Selected Poems*
James Den Boer, *Learning the Way*
James Den Boer, *Trying to Come Apart*
Norman Dubie, *Alehouse Sonnets*
Norman Dubie, *In the Dead of the Night*
Odysseus Elytis, *The Axion Esti*
John Engels, *The Homer Mitchell Place*
John Engels, *Signals from the Safety Coffin*
Abbie Huston Evans, *Collected Poems*
Brendan Galvin, *No Time for Good Reasons*
Gary Gildner, *Digging for Indians*
Gary Gildner, *First Practice*
Gary Gildner, *Nails*
Mark Halperin, *Backroads*
Michael S. Harper, *Dear John, Dear Coltrane*
Michael S. Harper, *Song: I Want a Witness*
Samuel Hazo, *Blood Rights*
Samuel Hazo, *Once for the Last Bandit: New and Previous Poems*
Samuel Hazo, *Quartered*
Gwen Head, *Special Effects*
Shirley Kaufman, *The Floor Keeps Turning*
Shirley Kaufman, *Gold Country*
Abba Kovner, *A Canopy in the Desert*
Paul-Marie Lapointe, *The Terror of the Snows: Selected Poems*
Larry Levis, *Wrecking Crew*
Jim Lindsey, *In Lieu of Mecca*
Tom Lowenstein, tr., *Eskimo Poems from Canada and Greenland*
Archibald MacLeish, *The Great American Fourth of July Parade*
Judith Minty, *Lake Songs and Other Fears*
James Moore, *The New Body*
Carol Muske, *Camouflage*
Thomas Rabbitt, *Exile*
Belle Randall, *101 Different Ways of Playing Solitaire and Other Poems*
Ed Roberson, *Etai-Eken*
Ed Roberson, *When Thy King Is A Boy*
Dennis Scott, *Uncle Time*
Herbert Scott, *Disguises*
Herbert Scott, *Groceries*
Richard Shelton, *Of All the Dirty Words*
Richard Shelton, *The Tattooed Desert*
Richard Shelton, *You Can't Have Everything*
David Steingass, *American Handbook*
David Steingass, *Body Compass*
Tomas Tranströmer, *Windows & Stones: Selected Poems*
Alberta T. Turner, *Learning to Count*
Marc Weber, *48 Small Poems*
David P. Young, *Sweating Out the Winter*

THE LIBRARY
ST. MARY'S COLLEGE OF MARYLAND
ST. MARY'S CITY, MARYLAND 20686